Vocabulary

Learn, discuss and research each word / name, use the definition pages to write your findings

Imhotep	Marie Van Brittan Brown
Medicine	Inventor
Teacher	Patent
Doctor	Intellectual Property
Architect	Home Security System
Egypt	Wireless System
Pyramid	Safety
Dynasty	Technology
Pharaoh	Communication
3rd Dynasty	
Dogon	Maurice Ashley
Tribe	Chess
Genius	Grandmaster
Sirius	King
Stars	Queen
Rituals	Strategy
Solar System	Tactics
Mali	Sacrifice
Africa	Checkmate
Ancestors	Check
Nommo	Stalemate

(ancestral spirits, sometimes referred to as
deities, worshipped by the Dogon people of Mali)

Vocabulary definition

Word:

Definition:

Name: _______________   Date: _______________

Imhotep 27th Century BCE

- Chief architect of the world's first monumental building, the Step Pyramid.
- Architect, Astrologist, Chief Minister to Djoser, Physician, considered an Egyptian Polymath, which is an individual who is an expert in many areas of learning.
- Developed medical texts describing 100 diseases and 48 injuries.
- Is still considered highly influential by other physicians.
- Treated diseases such as gout and appendicitis.
- Believed diseases occurred naturally and were not punishments or curses from the Gods or Spirits.
- He is the real father of medicine. Sir William Osler, one of the four founding professors of Johns Hopkins Hospital, said he is the *"first figure of a physician to clearly stand out from the mists of antiquity."*
- Became deified in 525 BCE as the God of wisdom and medicine.

The Dogons
c. 900-1400 - Present

- The Dogon are an ethnic group living in the central plateau region of Mali, in West Africa.
- They have their own systems of astronomy and calendrical measurements that have been passed down through oral history.
- The Dogon's rituals show a strong sense of harmony, One important ritual involves women praising men, men thanking women, and the young expressing appreciation for the old, and in return, the old recognizing the contributions of the young.
- The 1976, Robert K. G. Temple book, *The Sirius Mystery*, claims that the Dogon knew that Sirius is part of a binary star system, and had knowledge of its second star, Sirius B, a white dwarf completely invisible to the human eye. The West only made this discovery centuries later with telescopes and modern equipment.

Marie Van Brittan Brown
October 30, 1922 - February 2, 1999

- **Nurse, Inventor.**
- **In order to feel safer in her home, Marie created the first home security system in 1969, which consisted of peepholes, monitors, a camera, two-way microphone, and an alarm button.**
- **Through her home security system, Marie is also credited with helping to develop the first closed circuit television.**
- **Due to her invention, the National Scientists Committee honored her with an award.**
- **More than a dozen inventors cited Marie's patent for her security system for their own systems in 2013.**
- **New Scientist reported in 2016 that 100 million concealed closed circuit cameras were in operation because of Marie's invention.**

Maurice Ashley
March 6, 1966 - Present

- Jamaican-American chess grandmaster, author, commentator, app designer, puzzle inventor, and motivational speaker.
- On March 14, 1999, Ashley beat Adrian Negulescu to complete the requirements for the Grandmaster title. This made him the first black chess Grandmaster.
- Mentors young Chess players and is a part of Your Move Chess, a Saint Louis area after school program.
- On April 13, 2016, Ashley was inducted into the US Chess Hall of Fame.
- He was quoted *"African continent GMs do exist; but, according to the system of racial classification, I am the first Black GM in history... it matters, and doesn't matter, all at the same time."*

Handwriting

Name: _________________ *Date:* _________________

Imhotep Imhotep

Imhotep Imhotep

Imhotep Imhotep

Imhotep Imhotep

Imhotep Imhotep

Imhotep Imhotep

Handwriting

Name: _________________ Date: _________________

Pyramid Pyramid

Pyramid Pyramid

Pyramid Pyramid

Pyramid Pyramid

Pyramid Pyramid

Pyramid Pyramid

Handwriting

Name: _________________ *Date:* _________________

Dogon Dogon

Dogon
Dogon
Dogon
Dogon
Dogon

Dogon
Dogon
Dogon
Dogon
Dogon

Handwriting

Name: _________________   *Date:* _________________

<u>Solar System</u>

Solar System

Solar System

Solar System

Solar System

Solar System

Handwriting

Name: _______________ *Date:* _______________

Marie Van Brittan

Marie Van Brittan

Marie Van Brittan

Marie Van Brittan

Marie Van Brittan

Marie Van Brittan

Marie Van Brittan

SankofaClub.com

Handwriting

Inventor Inventor

Inventor Inventor

Inventor Inventor

Inventor Inventor

Inventor Inventor

Inventor Inventor

Handwriting

Name: _________________ *Date:* _________________

Maurice Ashley

Maurice Ashley

Maurice Ashley

Maurice Ashley

Maurice Ashley

Maurice Ashley

Maurice Ashley

Handwriting

Name: _________________ *Date:* _________________

Grandmaster

Grandmaster

Grandmaster

Grandmaster

Grandmaster

Grandmaster

Handwriting

Africa   Africa

Africa   Africa

Africa   Africa

Africa   Africa

Africa   Africa

Africa   Africa

Handwriting

Name: _________________ *Date:* _________________

Chess Chess

Chess Chess

Chess Chess

Chess Chess

Chess Chess

Chess Chess

Handwriting

Name: _______________ Date: _______________

Genius   Genius

Genius   Genius

Genius   Genius

Genius   Genius

Genius   Genius

Genius   Genius

SANKOFA KIDS

Green: Month 1   **SankofaClub.com**

Handwriting

Name: _________________ *Date:* _________________

Queen Queen

Queen Queen

Queen Queen

Queen Queen

Queen Queen

Queen Queen

Handwriting

Name: _________________ *Date:* _________________

Handwriting

Teacher   Teacher
Teacher   Teacher
Teacher   Teacher
Teacher   Teacher
Teacher   Teacher
Teacher   Teacher

Handwriting

Name: _________________ Date: _________________

Handwriting

Name: _________________ *Date:* _________________

Wireless Wireless
Wireless Wireless
Wireless Wireless
Wireless Wireless
Wireless Wireless
Wireless Wireless

Practice writing Your Name

Date: _______________

Dot-to-Dot

Imhotep was the architect of which structures?
Join the dots to find out!

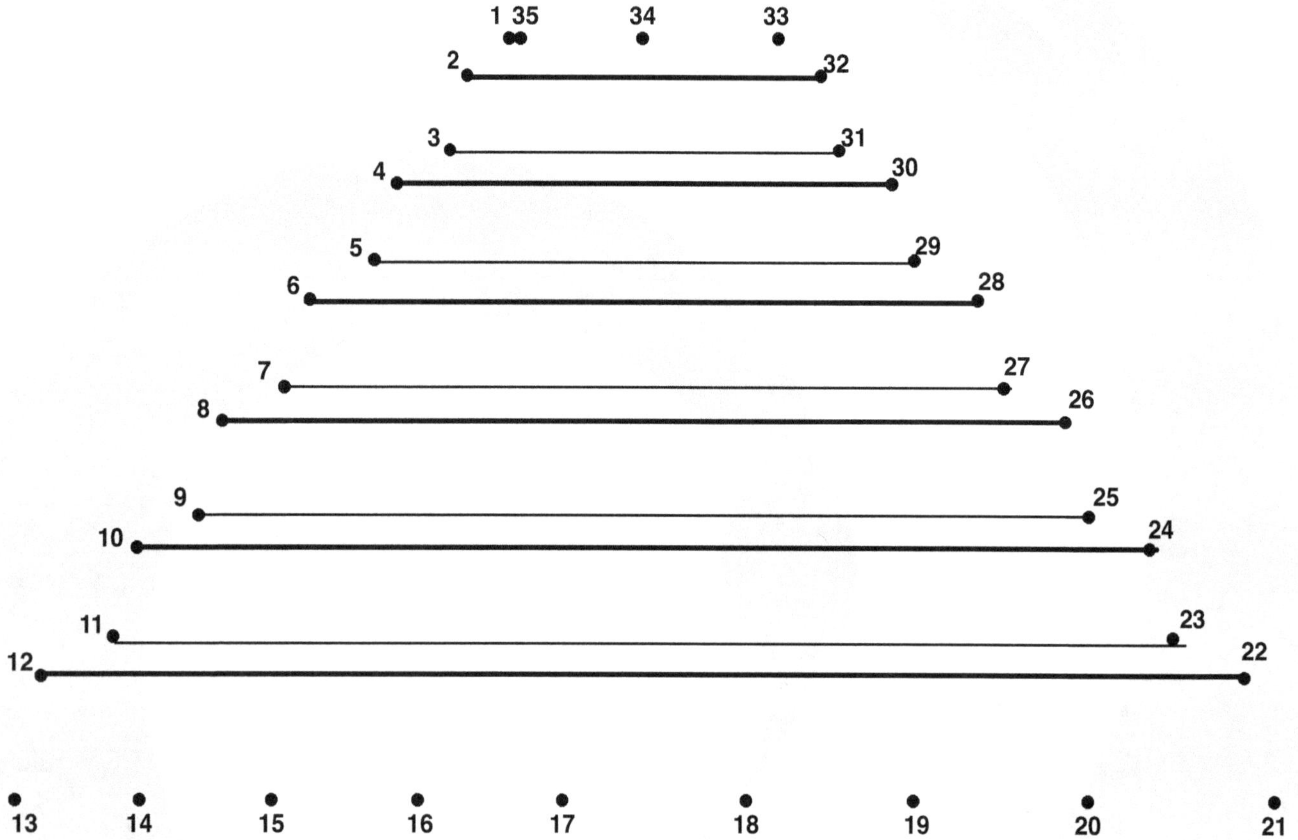

Dot-to-Dot

Which instrument is used to look at the stars?
Join the dots to find out!

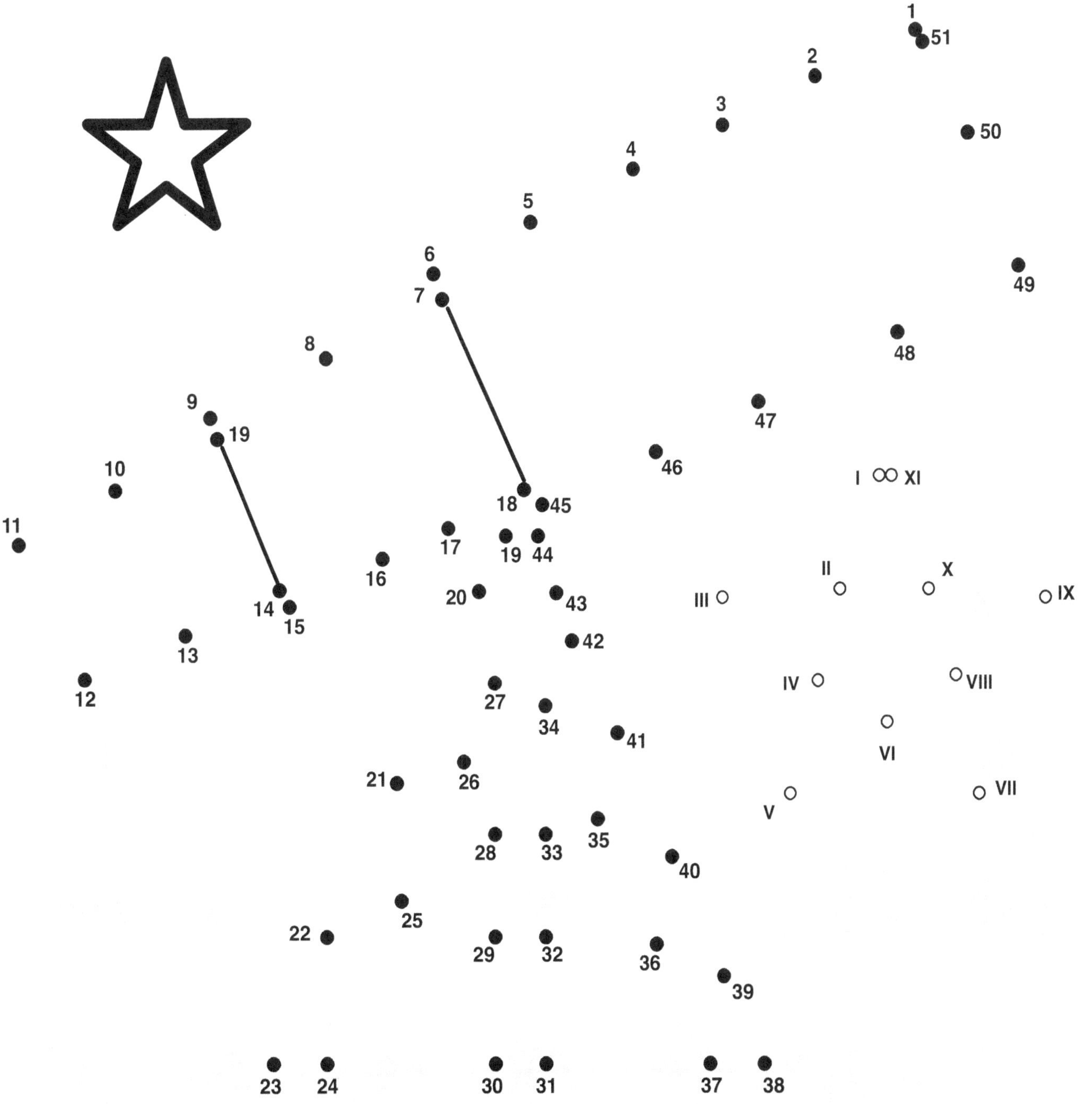

Dot-to-Dot

Maurice Ashley uses this game piece to compete.
Join the dots to find out!

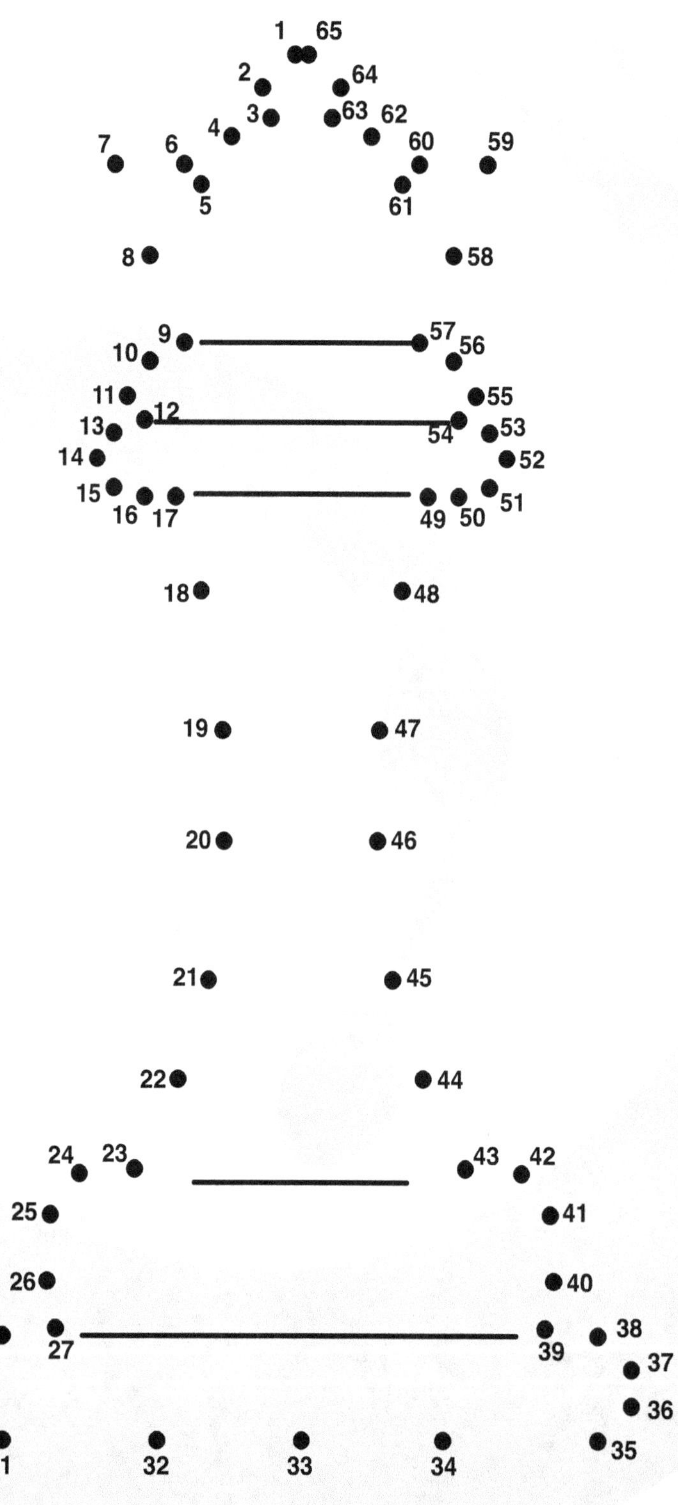

Star-to-Star

A constellation is a group of stars that make an imaginary outline or pattern in the sky. Most of them look like animals, mythological people or creatures. Join the numbers below to create these popular constellations.

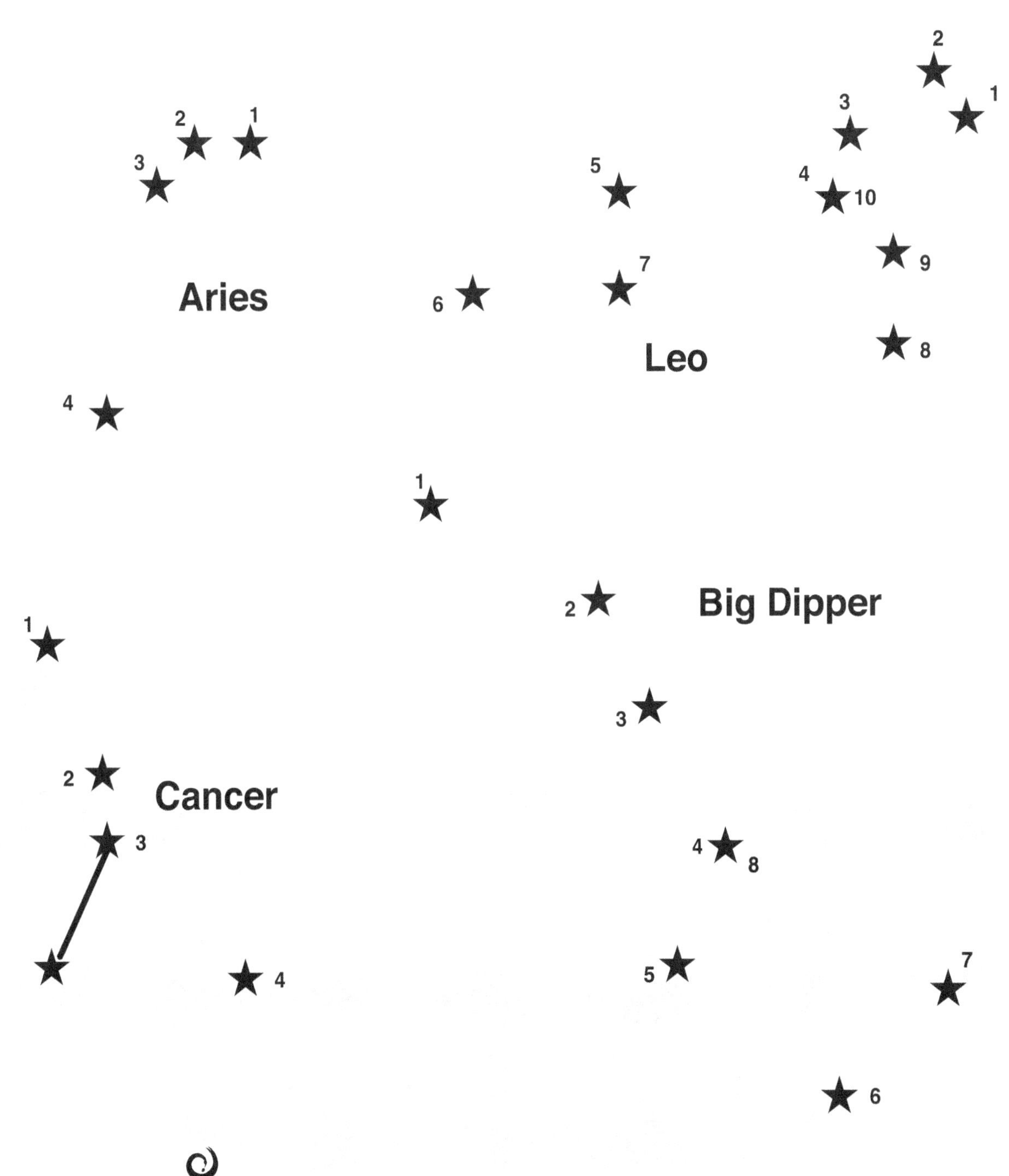

Coloring Exercises and Shape Recognition

Name: ________________ *Date:* ________________

This is a pyramid.
What shapes make up the pyramid?

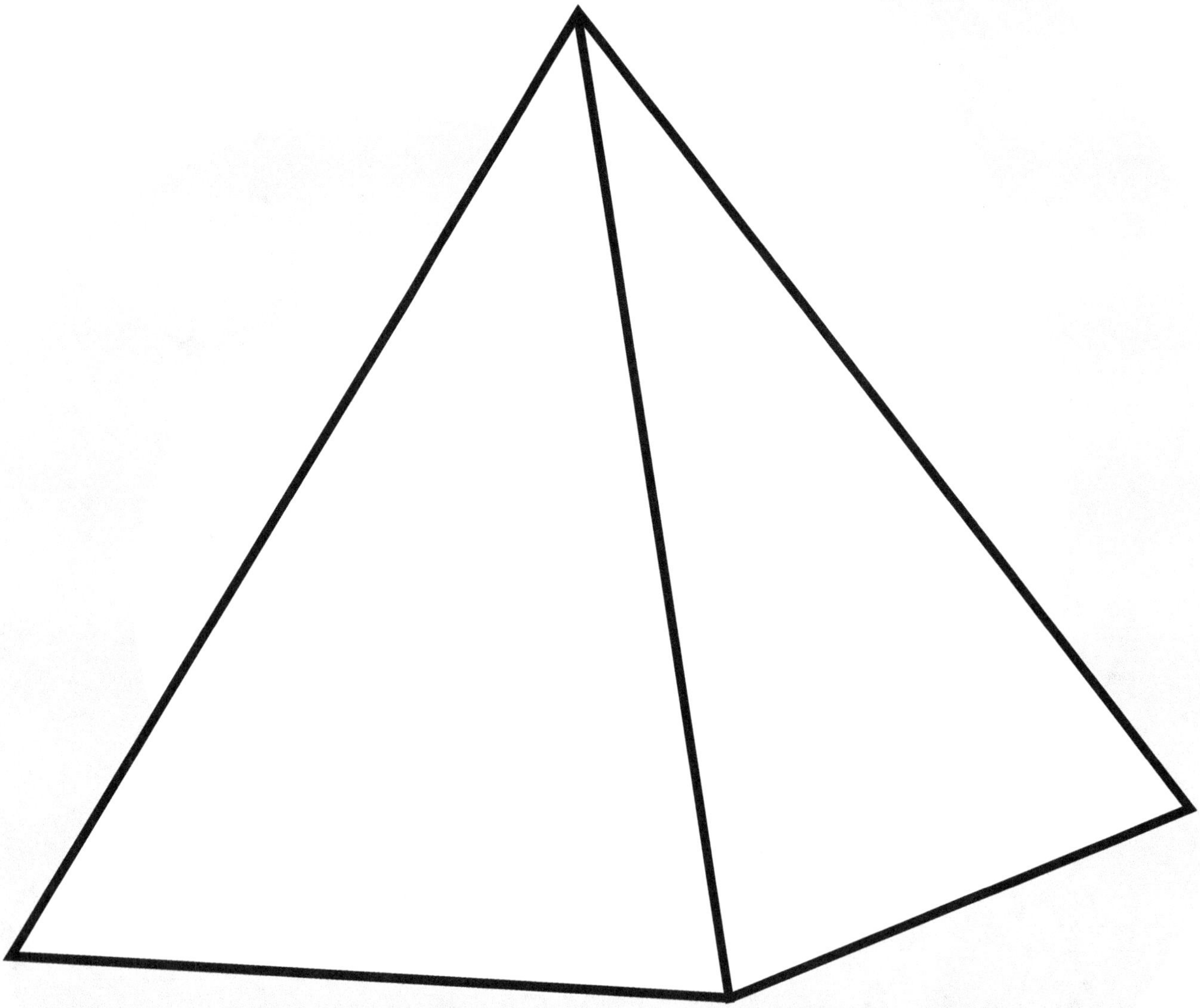

Impress the Pharaoh and decorate the pyramid with your favorite colors.

Coloring Exercises and Shape Recognition

Name: _________________ *Date:* _________________

This is a Egyptian symbol known as an Ankh. What shapes is it made from?

Decorate the Ankh with jewels and gold!

Coloring Exercises and Shape Recognition

Name: _________________ *Date:* _________________

This is made from rectangles and a circle. What is it?

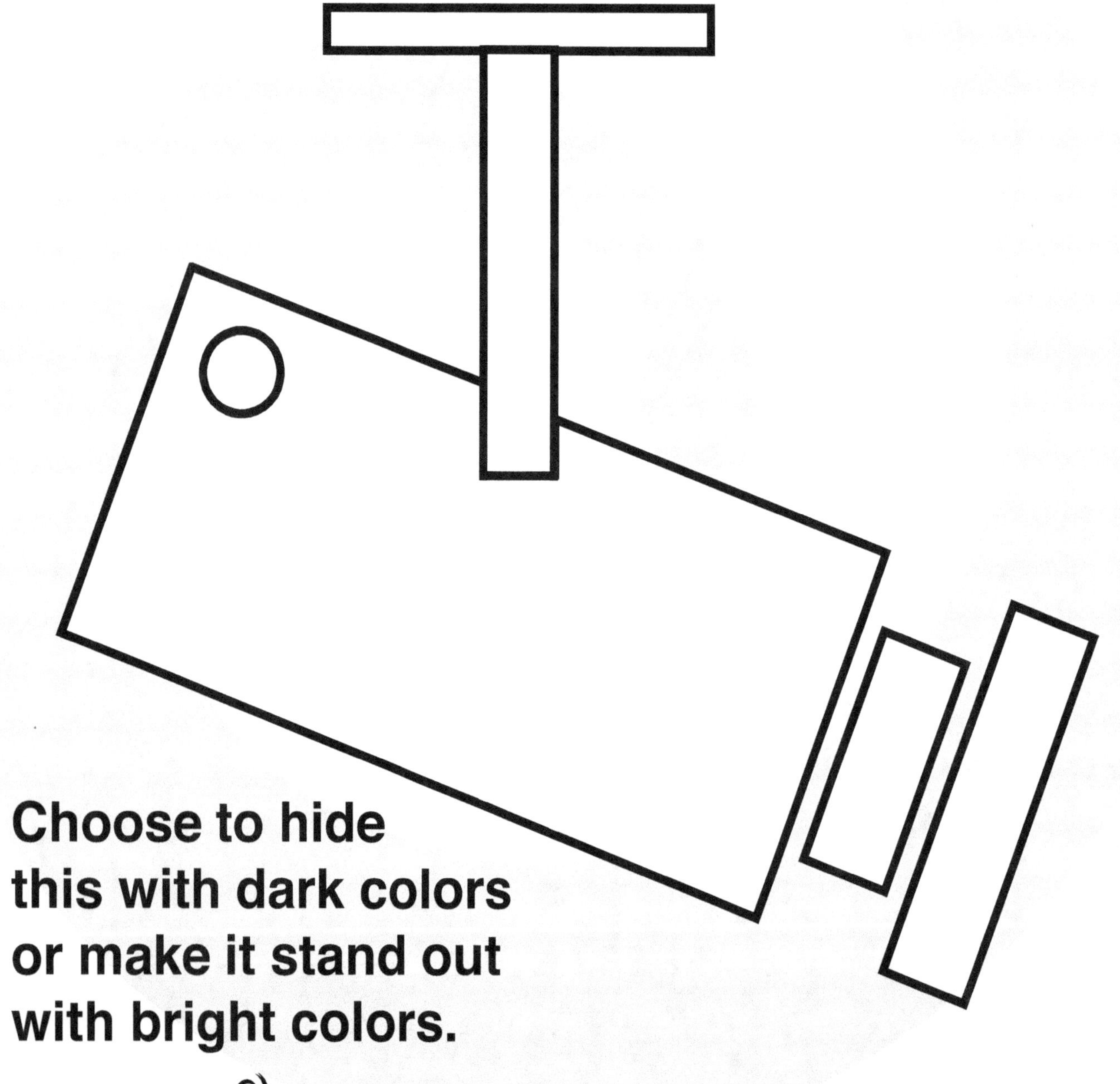

Choose to hide this with dark colors or make it stand out with bright colors.

Coloring Exercises and Shape Recognition

Name: _________________   *Date:* _________________

Chess pieces are very complex shapes. What shapes can you see in the pieces? What animal does the Knight look like?

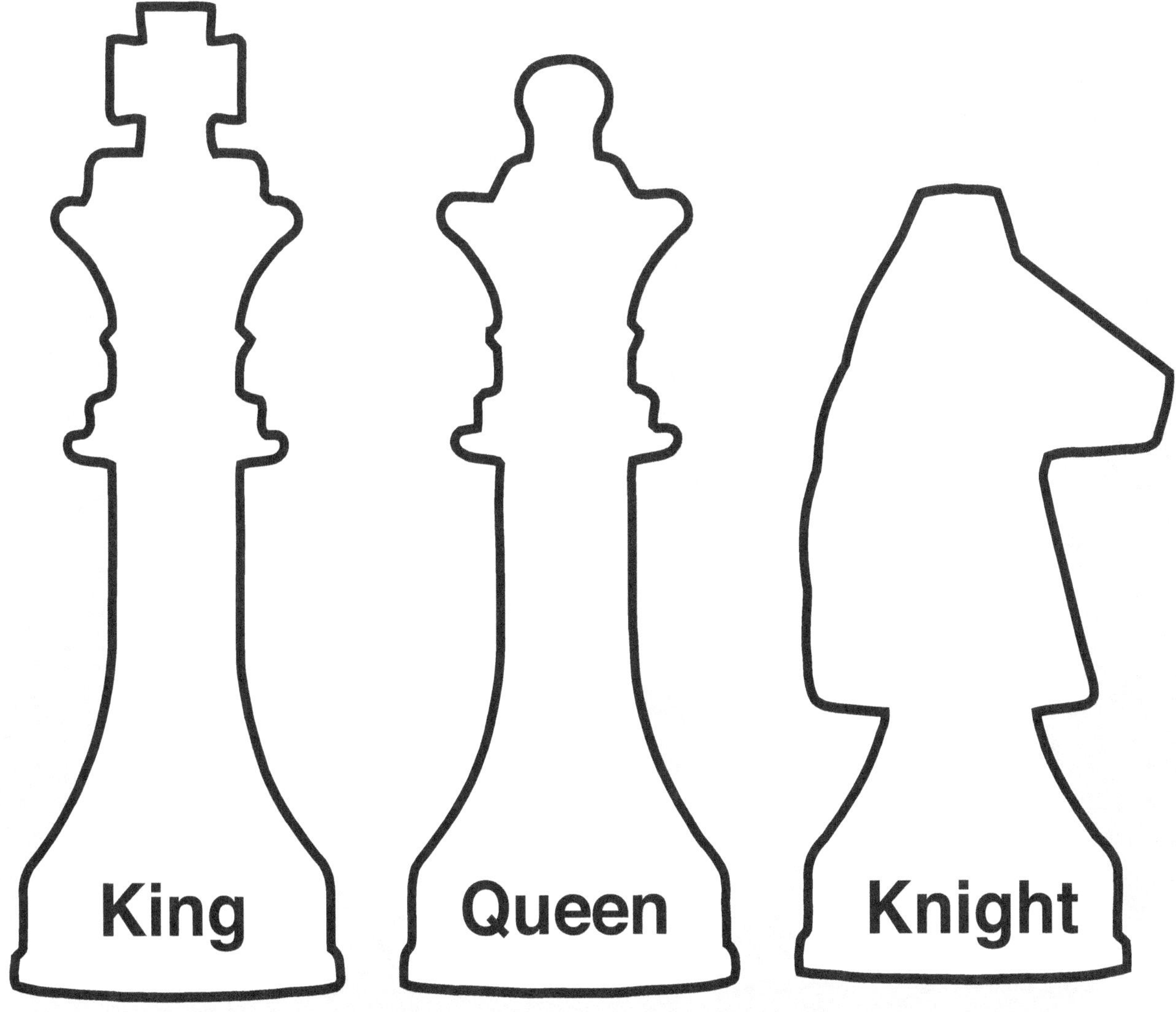

Chess pieces are normally Black or White but color these any color you like!

Help Imhotep reach the center of his largest pyramid.

Name: _________________ *Date:* _________________

The Dogons lost their Star System, help them find it. The stars are inside the circle.

Name: _________________________ *Date:* _________________________

Help Marie Van Brittan Brown turn on her security system before she leaves her home.

Name: _________________________ *Date:* _________________________

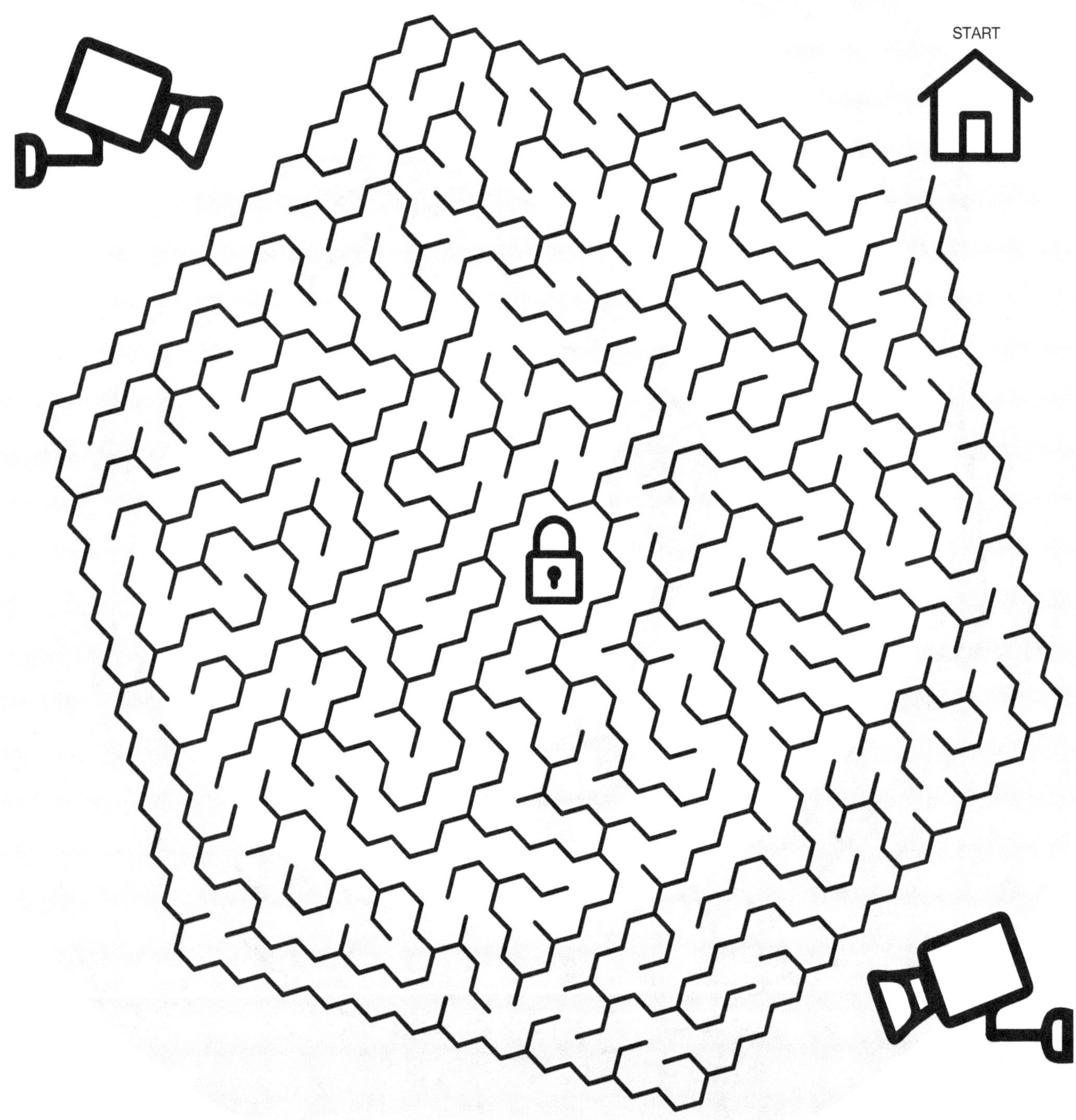

SANKOFA KIDS

Green: Month 1   SankofaClub.com

Can you help Maurice Ashley get to his chess piece?

Name: _________________ *Date:* _________________

Imhotep is trying to meet the Dogons.

Name: _______________ Date: _______________

SANKOFA KIDS

Maurice is figuring out his final and winning move in the tournament.

Name: _________________________ *Date:* _________________________

SOLUTION

Help Imhotep find the center of his pyramid.

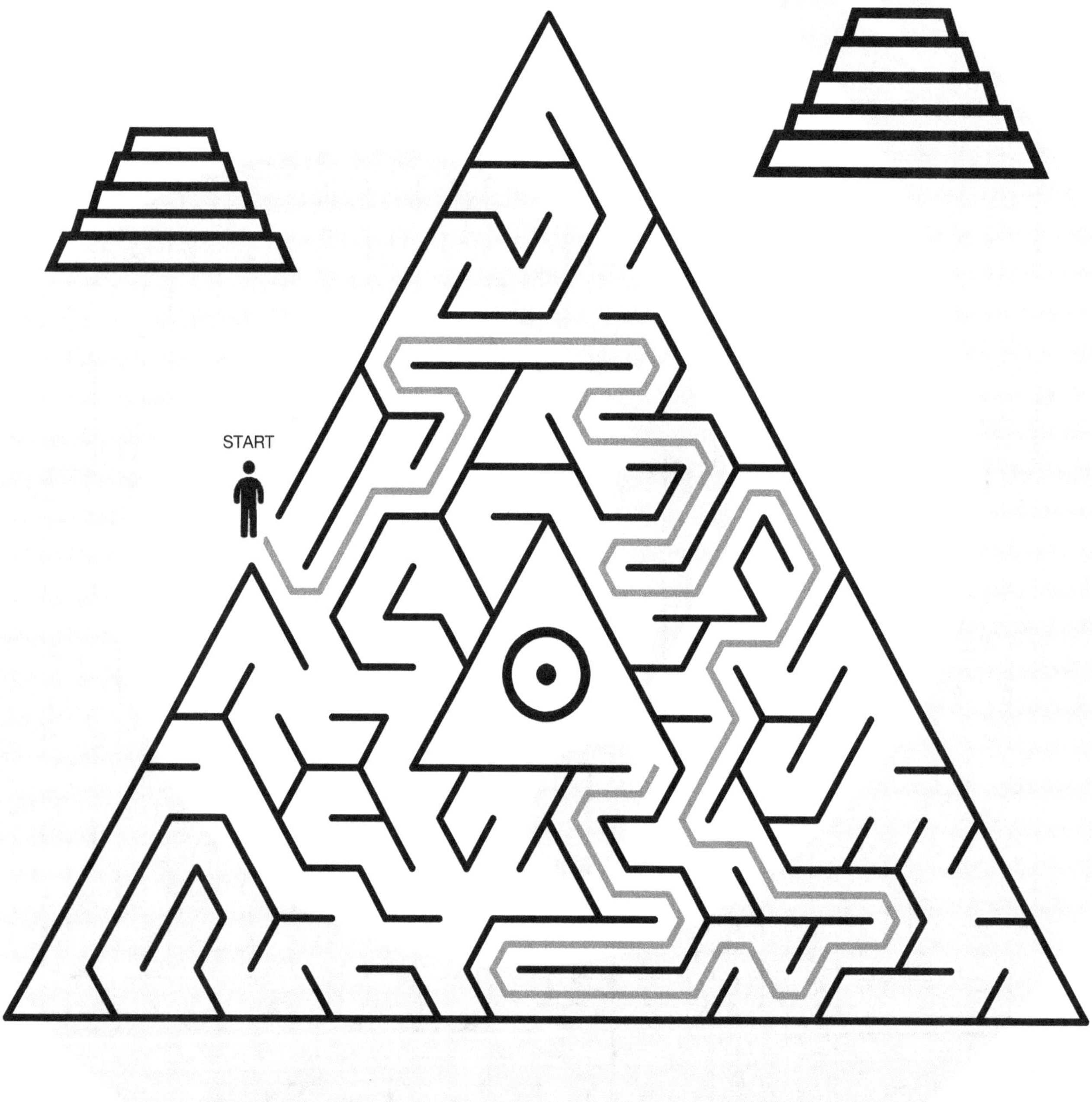

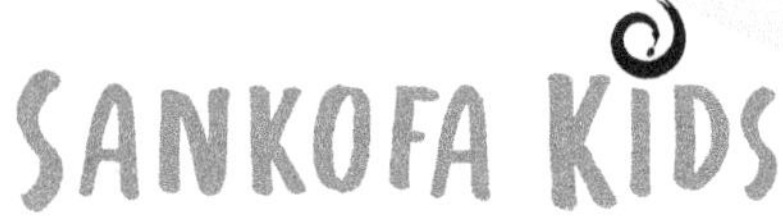

SOLUTION

The Dogons lost their Star System, help them find it. The stars are inside the circle.

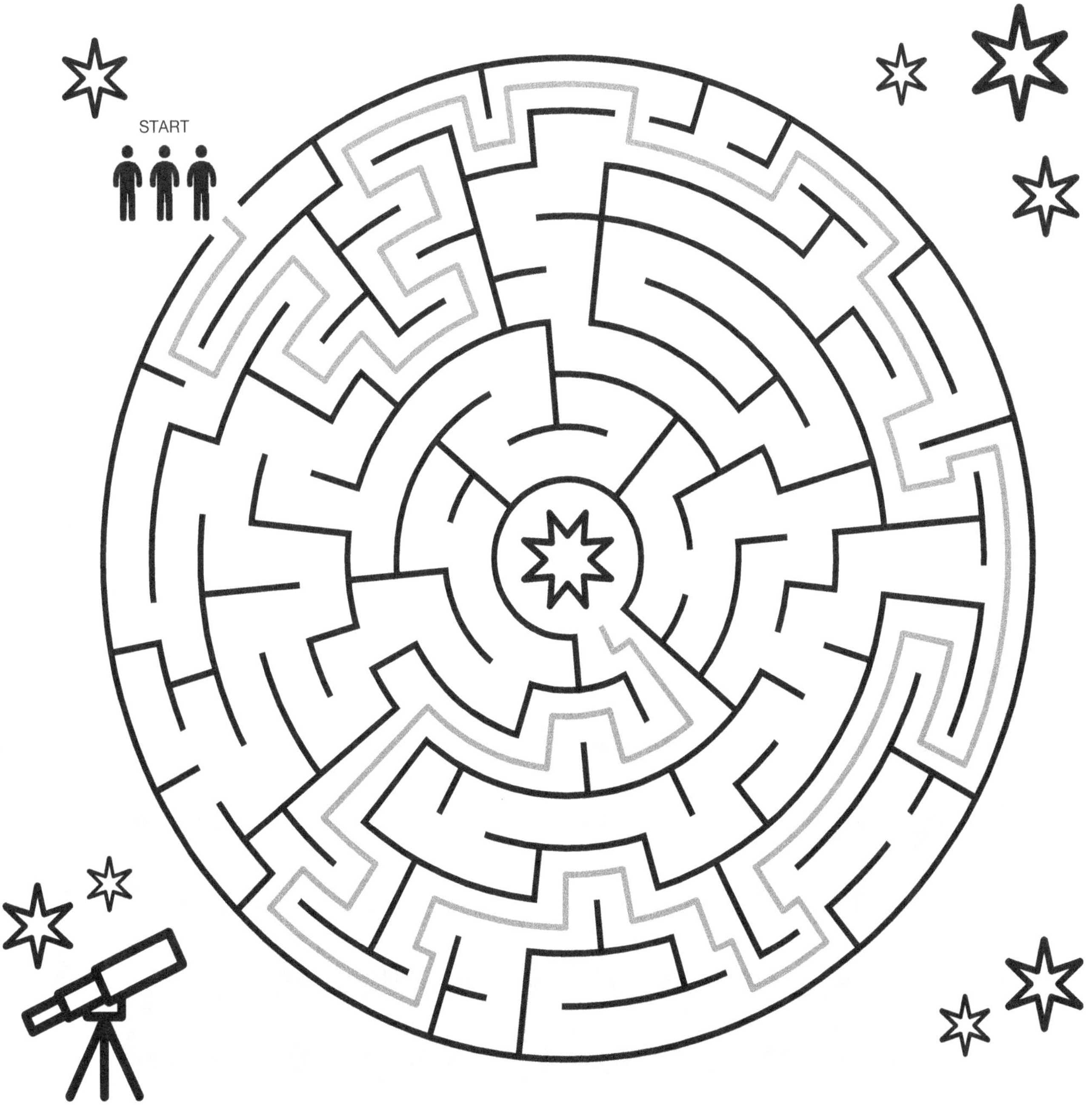

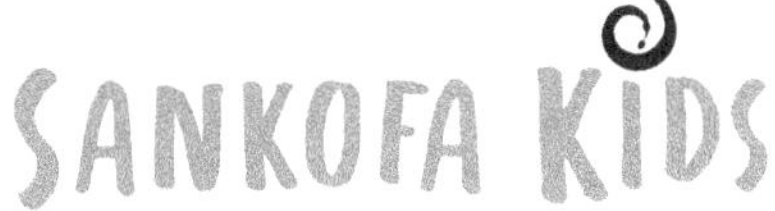

Help Marie Van Brittan Brown turn on her security system before she leaves her home.

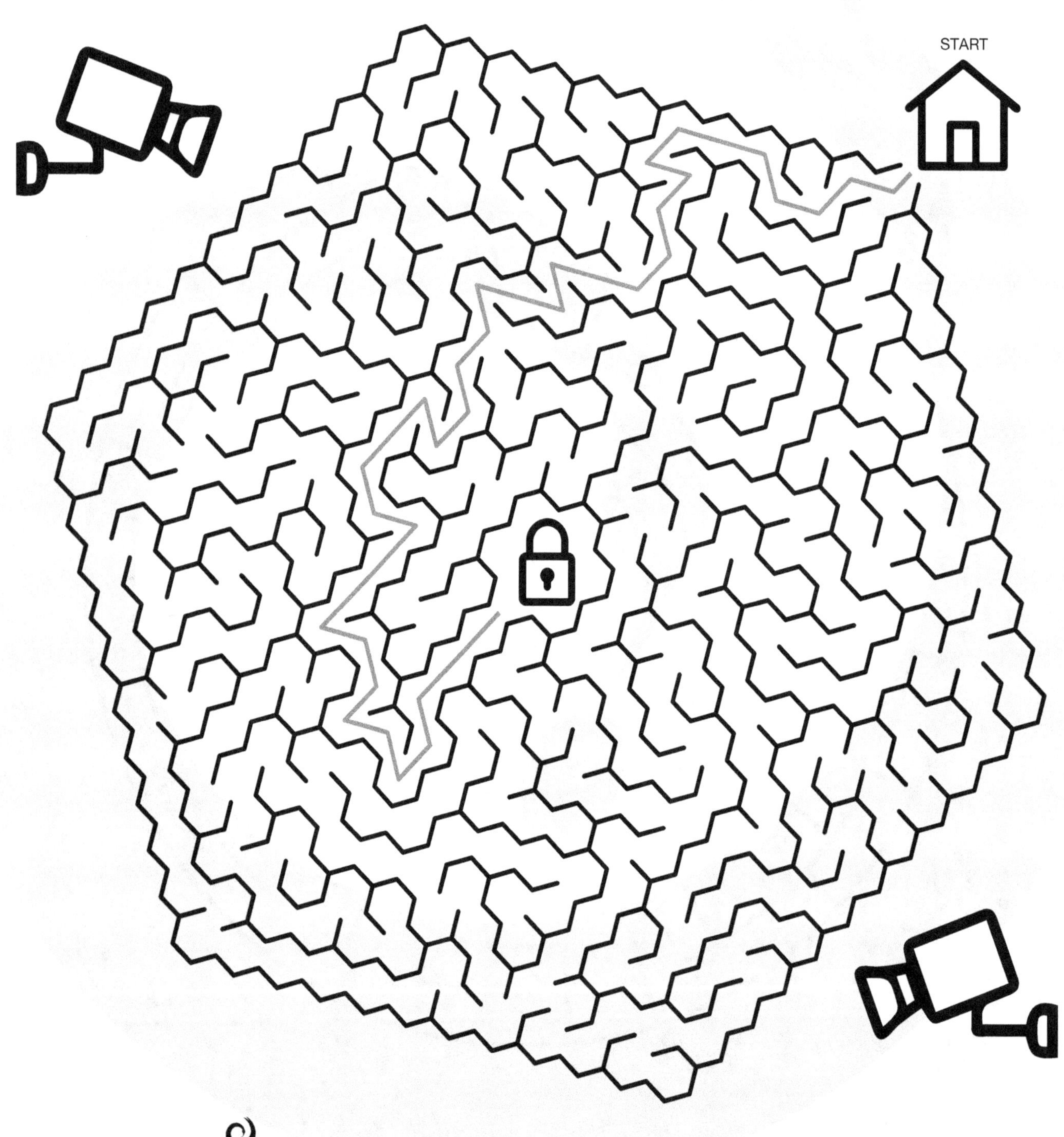

Can you help Maurice Ashley get to his chess piece?

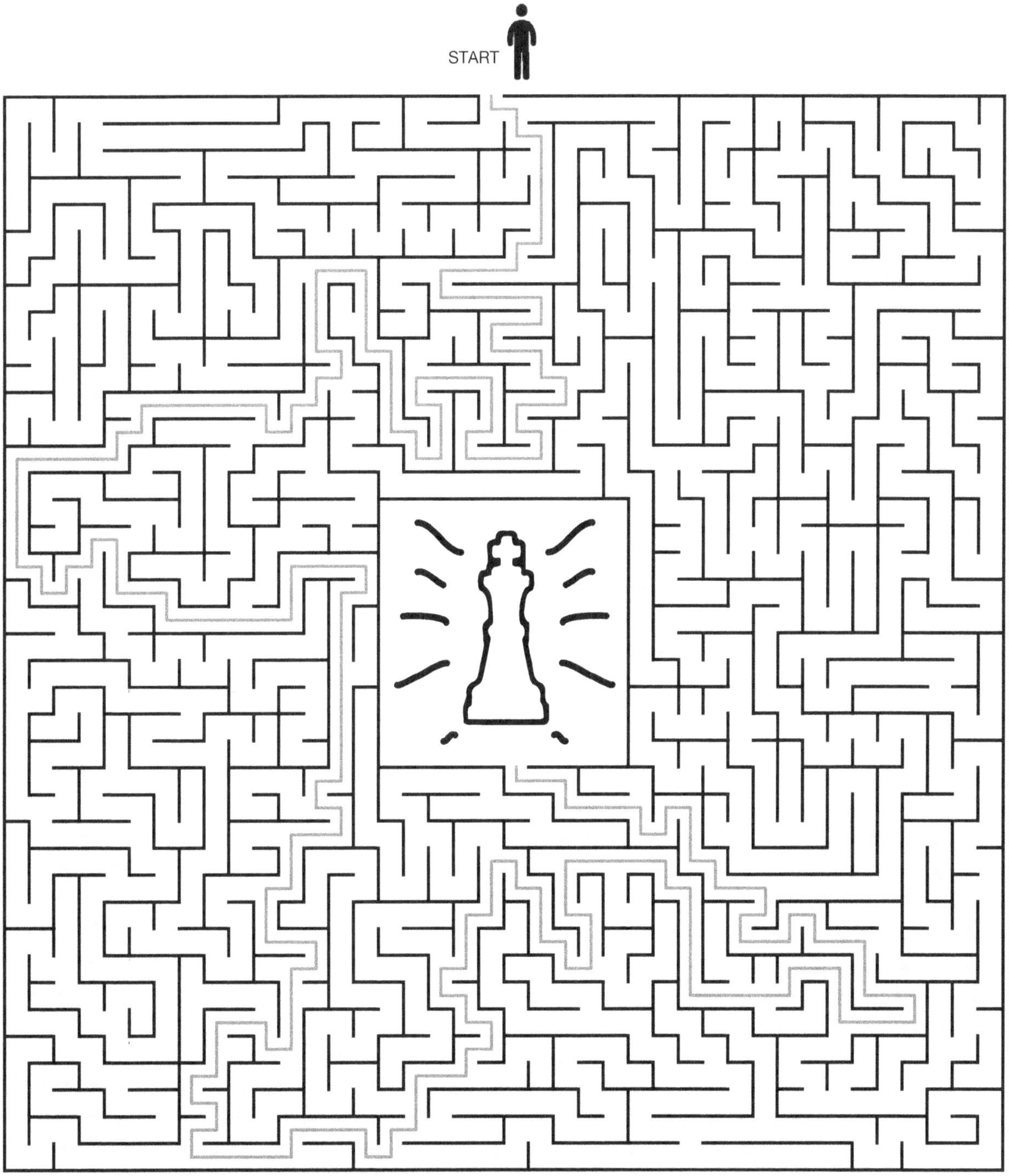

Imhotep is trying to meet the Dogons.

Maurice is figuring out his final and winning move in the tournament.

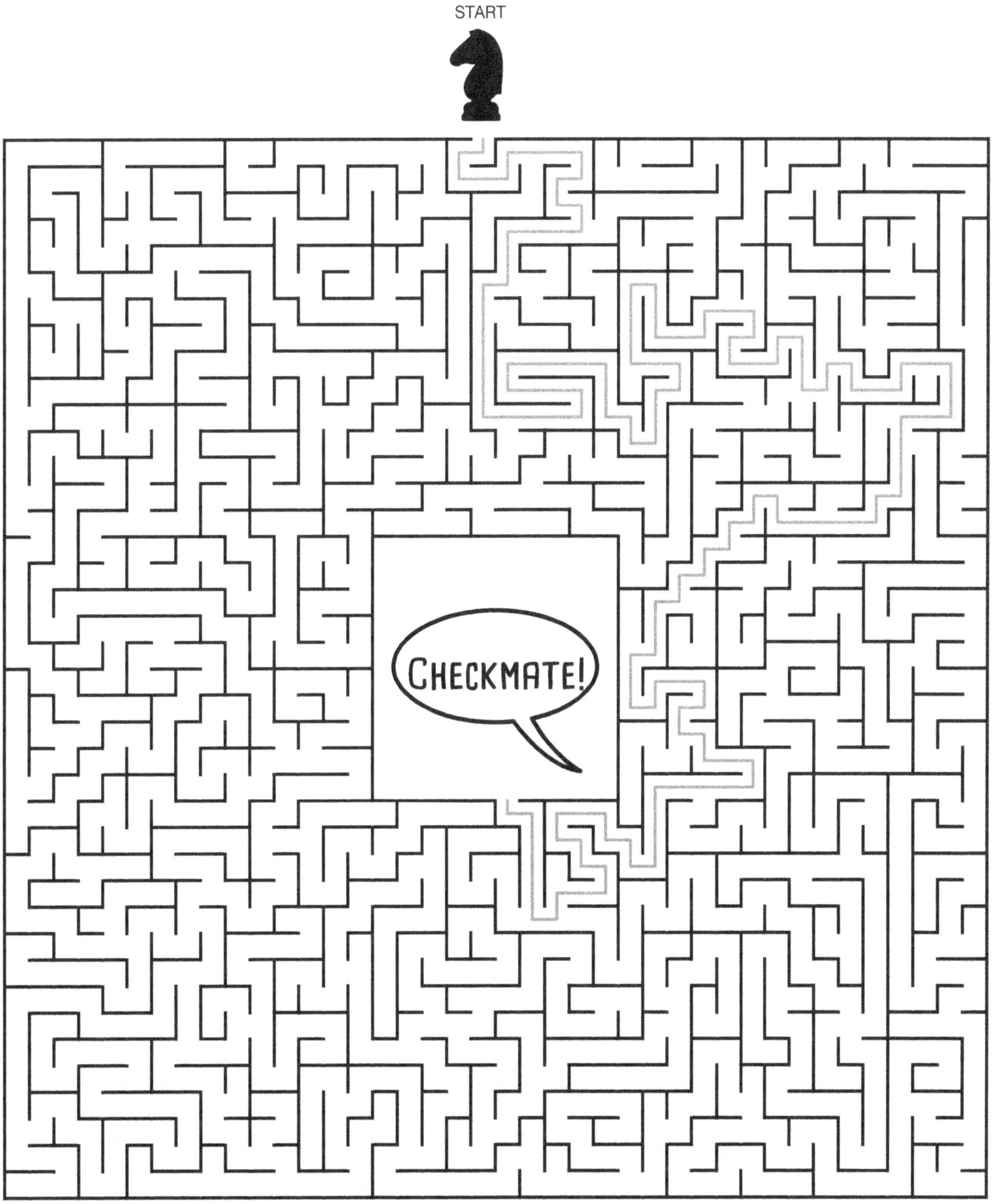

Word Shapes - Imhotep

Name: _______________ *Date:* _______________

Word List

Egypt   Imhotep   Doctor   Medicine   Architect   Teacher

Ancestors   Pharaoh   Dynasty   Africa   Pyramid   God

Word Shapes - Dogons

Name: _________________________ Date: _____________________

Word List

| Sirius | Genius | Dogon | Rituals | Stars | Tribe |
| Mali | Solar | Ancestors | Africa | System | Nommo |

SANKOFA KIDS

Word Shapes - Marie Van Brittan Brown

Name: ________________   *Date:* ________________

Word List

Word List.

Security	Marie	Patent	Home	Property	Inventor
Technology	Wireless	Brittan	Safety	Van	Camera

SANKOFA KIDS

Word Shapes - Maurice Ashley

Name: _________________ *Date:* _________________

Word List

King Master Maurice Strategy Queen Chess
Checkmate Tactics Stalemate Check Sacrifice Ashley

Wordsearch - Imhotep

Name: ________________ *Date:* ________________

											IMHOTEP
Z	Y	D	Y	N	A	S	T	Y	V		MEDICINE
P	M	E	D	I	C	I	N	E	K		TEACHER
H	K	V	R	E	H	C	A	E	T		DOCTOR
A	G	X	T	P	Y	G	E	C	M		ARCHITECT
R	F	I	M	H	O	T	E	P	C		EGYPT
A	A	N	U	Z	K	G	Z	W	Z		PYRAMID
O	T	C	E	T	I	H	C	R	A		DYNASTY
H	M	D	I	M	A	R	Y	P	A		PHARAOH
F	E	Y	R	O	T	C	O	D	R		
O	J	T	Y	M	W	Q	H	D	D		

SANKOFA KIDS

Wordsearch - Dogon

Name: _________________________ *Date:* _________________________

C	V	J	R	A	T	D	X	T	U
Z	S	X	L	I	U	R	Y	Y	R
V	S	R	T	N	T	U	I	X	J
S	W	O	O	S	S	U	H	B	M
N	U	G	L	T	U	D	A	W	E
I	O	I	A	A	S	I	M	L	T
D	L	R	N	P	R	E	R	L	S
T	S	A	N	E	H	F	C	I	Y
N	O	M	M	O	G	B	D	N	S
E	U	X	L	A	F	R	I	C	A

DOGON

TRIBE

GENIUS

SIRIUS

STARS

RITUALS

SOLAR

SYSTEM

MALI

AFRICA

ANCESTORS

NOMMO

Wordsearch - Marie Van Brittan Brown


```
N D Y T R E P O R P     VAN
A B R I T T A N I Z     BRITTAN
V I N V E N T O R S     INVENTOR
P A T E N T M B Y Y     PATENT
Y G O L O N H C E T     PROPERTY
Q Y T E F A S L D A     HOME
E M O H I N F I D N     SECURITY
D R S Y S T E M I W     SYSTEM
S E C U R I T Y L G     WIRELESS
H K W I R E L E S S     SAFETY
                        TECHNOLOGY
```

Wordsearch - Maurice Ashley

Name: _____________________   *Date:* _____________________

P	S	A	C	R	I	F	I	C	E		MAURICE
C	S	R	S	S	K	I	N	G	C		ASHLEY
S	A	E	T	S	V	X	O	H	J		CHESS
T	S	S	A	E	D	K	E	E	T		KING
R	H	K	L	H	F	C	D	C	A		STRATEGY
A	L	R	E	C	K	E	X	I	C		TACTICS
T	E	W	M	M	R	H	A	R	T		SACRIFICE
E	Y	W	A	I	X	C	F	U	I		CHECKMATE
G	G	T	T	P	N	C	A	A	C		CHECK
Y	E	W	E	N	T	B	E	M	S		STALEMATE

Wordsearch - All

Name: _________________ Date: _________________

F	S	D	R	I	O	I	E	E	A		MEDICINE
X	Y	G	O	W	W	A	I	B	E		TEACHER
T	E	R	T	C	P	E	R	I	N		DOCTOR
E	L	A	C	I	E	N	A	R	W		EGYPT
C	H	N	O	D	T	I	M	T	Y		DOGON
H	S	D	D	O	O	C	Y	S	T		TRIBE
N	A	M	S	G	H	I	I	P	E		GENIUS
O	A	A	M	O	M	D	N	G	F		STARS
L	N	S	C	N	I	E	V	E	A		AFRICA
O	C	T	E	C	E	M	E	N	S		ANCESTORS
G	E	E	B	G	H	U	N	I	R		MARIE
Y	S	R	E	A	L	S	T	U	T		INVENTOR
F	T	Q	M	F	P	R	O	S	P		SAFETY
K	O	E	I	R	S	A	R	D	Y		TECHNOLOGY
X	R	K	B	I	S	T	W	F	G		ASHLEY
R	S	G	X	C	N	S	N	Q	E		CHESS
L	E	T	E	A	C	H	E	R	B		GRANDMASTER
A	H	M	O	O	C	S	Q	H	Z		CHECK
W	K	F	U	C	H	E	C	K	C		

Word Scramble - Imhotep

Name: _________________ *Date:* _________________

| Imhotep | Teacher | Doctor | Egypt | Medicine | Pharaoh |
| Pyramid | Architect | 3rd Dynasty | Dynasty | | |

1. IHMETPO   _ m _ _ t _ _

2. NICEDIEM   _ _ _ _ c _ n _

3. CEAHRTE   _ e _ _ e _

4. CTODRO   _ o c _ _ _

5. HTTERACCI   _ _ c _ i _ _ _ _

6. YPGET   _ _ _ p _

7. MYPDRAI   _ _ r _ _ _ d

8. TASDYNY   _ _ _ a s _ _

9. PAAOHH R   _ _ _ _ a _ h

10. DYT3R DSAYN   _ _ _   _ _ n a s _ _

Word Scramble - Dogons

Name: _________________ *Date:* _________________

Ancestors	Rituals	Sirius	Mali	Stars	Tribe
Africa	Dogon	Genius	Nommo	Solar System	

1. D GONO   _ _ _ o _

2. ERBIT   _ r _ _ _

3. GISNUE   G _ _ _ u _

4. SIRSUI   _ _ r i _ _

5. TASRS   _ t _ _ _

6. IURALTS   _ _ t _ _ l _

7. LM SEOASSRTY   _ o _ _ r _ _ s _ _ _

8. LMAI   _ _ l _

9. AIAFRC   A _ _ _ _ a

10. RESNOTSAC   _ n _ _ s _ _ _ _

11. MONMO   _ _ _ m _

Word Scramble - Marie Van Brittan Brown

Name: ________________________ *Date:* ________________________

Home Security System Safety	Patent Technology	Wireless System Inventor	Marie Van Brittan Brown	Communication	Intellectual Property

1. thnocogely   _ _ c _ _ _ _ o _ y

2. ptneat   _ _ t _ _ t

3. irnovnet   I _ _ _ _ _ o _

4. t scuymeshoireytes m   _ o _ _ _ e _ _ _ i _ _ _ _ _ _ e _

5. mniicotcmanou   _ o m m _ _ _ _ _ _ _ _

6. bvrn ntbwr aoainmi trea   _ _ r _ _ _ a n _ _ _ _ _ _ _ _ _ _ w _

7. sreyeitmessl sw   _ _ _ _ _ _ _ s _ _ _ _ t e m

8. ytasfe   _ a _ e _ _

9. loeetltcepyrt ripnlua   I _ _ _ l l _ _ _ _ _ _ P _ _ _ _ _ t _

Word Scramble - Maurice Ashley

Name: ________________ *Date:* ________________

Tactics	Queen	Maurice Ashley	King	Grandmaster	Check
Stalemate	Checkmate	Strategy	Chess	Sacrifice	

1. ICRSMLH YEUAEA

   _ _ _ _ i _ _   _ s _ l _

2. SECSH

   _ _ _ s

3. SAETADNRMGR

   G _ _ _ d _ _ _ _ _ _

4. NIGK

   K _ _ _

5. UQEEN

   _ u _ _ _

6. GTSATYRE

   _ _ _ _ _ _ g y

7. CTTCSIA

   _ _ _ t i _ _

8. ICRSFECAI

   S _ _ _ _ _ i _ _

9. EHAMCTCEK

   _ h _ _ k _ _ _ _

10. CEHCK

    _ _ _ _ k

11. TASMTEEAL

    _ _ _ l _ m _ _ _

Word Scramble - Imhotep Solution

Name: ________________________   *Date:* ________________________

| Imhotep | Teacher | Doctor | Egypt | Medicine | Pharaoh |
| Pyramid | Architect | 3rd Dynasty | Dynasty | | |

1. IHMETPO — Imhotep

2. NICEDIEM — Medicine

3. CEAHRTE — Teacher

4. CTODRO — Doctor

5. HTTERACCI — Architect

6. YPGET — Egypt

7. MYPDRAI — Pyramid

8. TASDYNY — Dynasty

9. PAAOHH R — Pharaoh

10. DYT3R DSAYN — 3rd Dynasty

Word Scramble - Dogons Solution

Name: ________________ *Date:* ________________

Ancestors	Rituals	Sirius	Mali	Stars	Tribe
Africa	Dogon	Genius	Nommo	Solar System	

1. D GONO   Dogon

2. ERBIT   Tribe

3. GISNUE   Genius

4. SIRSUI   Sirius

5. TASRS   Stars

6. IURALTS   Rituals

7. LM SEOASSRTY   Solar System

8. LMAI   Mali

9. AIAFRC   Africa

10. RESNOTSAC   Ancestors

11. MONMO   Nommo

Word Scramble - Marie Van Brittan Brown Solution

Name: _________________ *Date:* _________________

Home Security System	Patent	Wireless System	Marie Van Brittan Brown	Communication	Intellectual Property
Safety	Technology	Inventor			

1. thnocogely — Technology

2. ptneat — Patent

3. irnovnet — Inventor

4. t scuymeshoireytes m — Home Security System

5. mniicotcmanou — Communication

6. bvrn ntbwr aoainmi trea — Marie Van Brittan Brown

7. sreyeitmessl sw — Wireless System

8. ytasfe — Safety

9. loeetltcepyrt ripnlua — Intellectual Property

Word Scramble - Maurice Ashley Solution

Name: _________________ *Date:* _________________

Tactics	Queen	Maurice Ashley	King	Grandmaster	Check
Stalemate	Checkmate	Strategy	Chess	Sacrifice	

1. ICRSMLH YEUAEA — Maurice Ashley
2. SECSH — Chess
3. SAETADNRMGR — Grandmaster
4. NIGK — King
5. UQEEN — Queen
6. GTSATYRE — Strategy
7. CTTCSIA — Tactics
8. ICRSFECAI — Sacrifice
9. EHAMCTCEK — Checkmate
10. CEHCK — Check
11. TASMTEEAL — Stalemate

Crossword - Imhotep

Name: _________________   *Date:* _________________

Across

1. An ancient kingdom
2. A builder
3. Shaped like a triangle

Down

1. Father of medicine
2. Used to heal people
3. Helps people learn
4. Country in Africa

Crossword - Dogons

Name: _________________ Date: _________________

Across

1. collection of planets and moons moving around the sun
2. Birthplace of mankind
3. Relatives from long ago
4. Ancestral spirits

Down

1. A very smart person
2. A grouping of stars
3. A series of actions performed
4. Country in west Africa
5. A group of people

Crossword - Marie Van Brittan Brown

Name: _________________________ Date: _________________________

Across

1. Created the home security system.
2. No wires needed

Down

1. An idea / product / invention that someone has created.
2. Monitors your home for danger
3. Feeling protected
4. An easy or better way to do something
5. Exchanging information or news

Crossword - Maurice Ashley

Name: _________________ *Date:* _________________

Across

1. Black Grandmaster in chess
2. In chess, when a King is threatened and can't move

Down

1. A board game of strategic skill for two players, played on a checkered board
2. A chess player of the highest class
3. Most powerful piece in chess match
4. A plan of action
5. An action for a specific purpose
6. To give something up
7. In chess, when a King is in danger
8. A tie in chess

Crossword - Imhotep Solution

Name: _________________ *Date:* _________________

Across

1. 3rddynasty
2. architect
3. pyramid

Down

1. imhotep
2. medicine
3. teacher
4. egypt

Crossword - Dogons Solution

Name: _____________________ *Date:* _____________________

Across

1. solarsystem
2. africa
3. ancestors
4. nommo

Down

1. genius
2. sirius
3. rituals
4. mali
5. tribe

Crossword - Marie Van Brittan Brown Solution

Across

1. marievanbrittanbrown
2. wirelesssystem

Down

1. intellectualproperty
2. homesecuritysystem
3. safety
4. technology
5. communication

Crossword - Maurice Ashley Solution

Name: ________________ *Date:* ________________

Across

1. mauriceashley
2. checkmate

Down

1. chess
2. grandmaster
3. queen
4. strategy
5. tactics
6. sacrifice
7. check
8. stalemate

Figure out the missing symbols in these images. Each symbol should appear in every row one time only.

Figure out the missing symbols in these images. Each symbol should appear in every row one time only.

Figure out the missing symbols in these images. Each symbol should appear in every row one time only.

Figure out the missing symbols in these images. Each symbol should appear in every row one time only.

SOLUTION

Puzzle 1

Puzzle 2

Puzzle 3

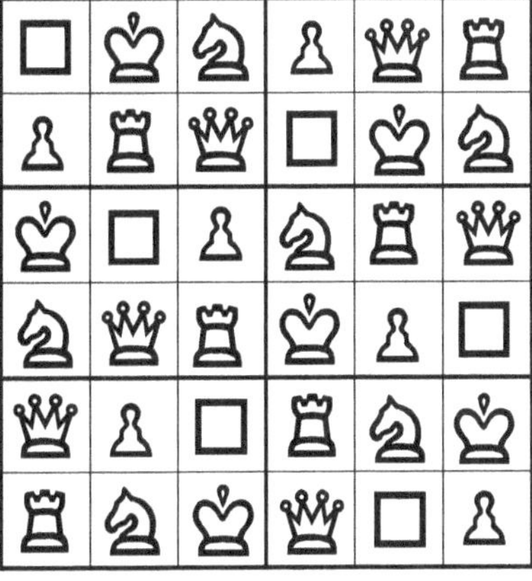

Puzzle 4

Writing Assignment

Imhotep has been asked by the Pharaoh to build a new pyramid with a unique design. Describe what this building will look like.

Writing Assignment

How do you think the Dogon people knew so much about the stars? Write down your story below.

SANKOFA KIDS

Writing Assignment

Marie Van Brittan Brown is testing her new security camera. Describe what she can see.

Writing Assignment

**Maurice Ashley's favorite game is Chess.
Describe your favorite game.**